THE ART OF 3D ANIMATION

A COMPREHENSIVE GUIDE TO CRAFTING SPECTACULAR VISUALS

SUBHASH CHAUDHARY

Made with ❤ on the Notion Press Platform
www.notionpress.com

This book is dedicated to the pioneers of 3D animation, who dedicated their lives to advancing the art form and introducing it to the world. To those who sacrificed their time and energy to create something special, thank you for your hard work and dedication. Without you, this book would not exist.

Contents

Foreword *vii*

Preface *ix*

Acknowledgements *xi*

Prologue *xiii*

1. History Of 3d Animation 1
2. Basic Principles Of 3d Animation 3
3. Character Design 5
4. Storyboarding 7
5. Modeling 9
6. Texturing And Lighting 11
7. Animation 13
8. Rendering And Compositing 15
9. Sound Design 17

Conclusion 19

Foreword

Animation has come a long way since its humble beginnings in the late 19th century. What was once a quiet and simplistic form of entertainment has now become an incredibly popular, vibrant and dynamic art form with incredible potential.

The Art of 3D Animation is a comprehensive guide to the exciting world of 3D animation. From its earliest days to the modern techniques used today, this book covers everything you need to know to create stunning 3D animations.

With easy-to-understand explanations and detailed examples, this book is the perfect resource for anyone looking to take their animation skills to the next level.

The Art of 3D Animation is an invaluable resource for aspiring animators and professionals alike. Whether you're a beginner or a veteran, this book provides the essential knowledge and tools to bring your 3D creations to life.

With this book, you'll be able to craft characters, stories, worlds and more easily, allowing you to create stunning 3D animations that captivate your audience. The Art of 3D Animation is an essential guide for anyone interested in the art of 3D animation.

I highly recommend it to anyone looking to explore the exciting world of 3D animation and bring their unique vision to life.

Preface

It is my pleasure to bring you The Art of 3D Animation. In this book, you will learn the fundamentals of 3D animation and how to apply them to create visually stunning artwork.

From the basics of modeling and texturing to the intricacies of character animation and rendering, I will walk you through the entire 3D animation process.

You will also explore the different animation software available and learn how to choose the right tools for your project.

I will also provide guidance on how to optimize your workflow and how to troubleshoot common issues.

Whether you are a beginner or a seasoned professional, you will find The Art of 3D Animation to be an invaluable resource. If you are looking to take your 3D animation skills to the next level, this is the book for you. Happy animating!

Sincerely,

Subhash Chaudhary

Acknowledgements

I would like to thank all the people who helped me in writing this book.

Firstly, I would like to thank my editor, who guided me throughout the entire process and provided invaluable advice.

I would also like to thank my friends and family who supported me throughout the entire process.

I would like to thank the various software developers and professionals in the 3D animation industry who, through their work and advice, helped shape the contents of this book.

Finally, I would like to thank all the readers who have taken the time to read this book. Your interest and feedback are invaluable to me.

Prologue

Once upon a time, the art of 3D animation was the realm of only the most talented and creative artists. The technology needed to create dynamic and realistic 3D images was expensive and difficult to use. But over time, 3D animation software and hardware have become more accessible and easier to use.

The Art of 3D Animation is a comprehensive guide to creating stunning and professional 3D animations. It covers the basics of 3D animation and provides detailed instructions for creating realistic and dynamic 3D images. It will also explore the power of 3D animation software and hardware, and show how to make the most of these tools.

This book is intended for all levels of 3D animators, from beginners who are just starting out, to experienced professionals. With the help of this book, you can become a master of 3D animation and create breathtaking 3D images. So, let's get started!

CHAPTER ONE

History of 3D Animation

The history of 3D animation began in the early 1950s when the first 3D animation was created using a technique known as stop-motion animation. This technique involved using miniature objects and puppets photographed one frame at a time and then edited together to create the illusion of movement. This technique was used in various films, including the classic film King Kong.

In the late 1960s, computer graphics began to be used for animation. This technology allowed for more complex and realistic visuals than the traditional stop-motion technique. Computer graphics allowed for the creation of 3D animated characters and environments, as well as the use of computer-generated special effects. The first computer-generated 3D animation was created in 1972 for a movie called Futureworld.

In the 1980s, new techniques were developed to create 3D animation. One of the most popular techniques was called keyframe animation, which allowed animators to create realistic motion by creating a series of keyframes, which could then be linked together to create a fluid motion. This technique created some iconic animated films, such as The Lion King and Toy Story.

In the 1990s, 3D animation began to be used for more than just movies. Video games began to use 3D animation to create realistic and immersive game worlds. This was a huge leap forward for the gaming industry, allowing for more complex and engaging experiences.

Today, 3D animation has become a staple in the entertainment industry. It is used in movies, television, video games, and virtual reality experiences. 3D animation is used to create believable and immersive worlds and provide stunning visuals for viewers to enjoy.

CHAPTER TWO

Basic Principles of 3D Animation

3D animation is an art form that uses computer generated images to create realistic and dynamic visuals. This type of animation can be used to create a wide variety of effects, from realistic environments to fantastical creatures and objects.

In order to create 3D animation, animators must understand the fundamental principles of animation, as well as the techniques used to create a convincing 3D scene. The principles of animation are the same for all types of animation, but 3D animation has its own unique set of rules.

The first principle is the use of timing. Timing is important because it helps to emphasize certain movements and create a sense of fluidity. This is achieved by adjusting the number of frames per second (FPS) and the length of each frame.

The second principle of 3D animation is motion. Motion is essential in creating believable characters, objects, and environments. Animators must be able to create realistic and believable movement by applying forces, acceleration, and timing.

The third principle is weight. Weight is the amount of force that a character or object exerts on the surface or environment. This is important because it helps to create a sense of realism and believability.

The fourth principle is the use of staging. Staging is the process of creating and arranging objects, characters, and environments to create a composition that enhances the story. This is done to create a sense of realism and to draw the viewer into the scene.

The fifth principle is exaggeration. Exaggeration is used to create an impact on the viewer and to make the scene more dynamic. This is often done by exaggerating the size, shape, and movement of characters and objects.

Finally, the sixth principle is anticipation. Anticipation is used to create suspense and to draw the viewer's attention to a certain part of the scene. This is done by making objects or characters move in a certain way before an action takes place.

These are the basic principles of 3D animation. By understanding and incorporating these principles into your work, you can create dynamic and believable 3D scenes.

CHAPTER THREE

Character Design

Character design is an integral part of the animation process and is arguably one of the most important elements of any 3D animation project. The characters you create will be the focus of the story, and their design should reflect the tone and theme of the animation. Good character design is essential for creating believable and memorable characters that will engage your audience.

The first step in character design is to create a concept sketch. This sketch should be rough and provide a basic idea of what your character will look like. It should include basic details such as the character's size and shape, facial features, clothing, and hairstyle. Once you have a concept sketch, you can begin to refine the design by adding more details and refining the proportions.

When designing a character, it is important to consider the character's personality and how it will be conveyed through their design. Every character you create should have their own unique look and attitude. Pay attention to the lines, curves, and shapes of the character's face, body, and clothing to convey personality traits.

It is also important to consider the character's movements and how they will be animated. Pay attention to the balance and weight of the character, as well as how their clothing will move and flow. Think about how each action your character takes will be animated and how it will look on screen.

Finally, consider the character's environment. How will the character interact with their environment? Are they a part of a larger scene or a single character in an isolated environment? Think about the lighting and how it will affect the character's look and feel.

Character design is an important part of any 3D animation project. It is essential to create believable and engaging characters that will draw in your audience and tell the story you want to tell. With careful planning and attention to detail, you can create characters that are unique and memorable.

CHAPTER FOUR

Storyboarding

Storyboarding is an essential part of the 3D animation process, as it helps to plan out and visualize the animation before any actual animation takes place. Storyboards provide a blueprint for the animator to follow, as well as a way to communicate the story to other members of the animation team. In this chapter, we will discuss the basics of storyboarding and how it applies to 3D animation.

First, let's talk about what a storyboard is. A storyboard is essentially a comic-strip-like outline of a story. It displays a series of visual frames that depict the actions, dialogue, and other elements of the story in order. The storyboard breaks down the story into individual shots, or scenes. This allows the animator to plan out the action and scenes in a sequence, and to get a better understanding of the overall scope of the animation.

When it comes to 3D animation, the storyboard serves a similar purpose. It helps the animator to plan out the action, movements, and camera angles of the animation. It also allows the animator to plan out how the animation will be rendered, such as which rendering engine will be used, what lighting and shading effects will be used, and which materials will be used. Now that we understand what a storyboard is, let's talk about how to create one.

The best way to create a storyboard for 3D animation is to use a software program. There are many different software programs available that are specifically designed for 3D animation storyboarding. These programs allow you to create a storyboard quickly and easily, and they come with features such as scene-building tools, camera and lighting controls, and the ability to preview the animation in real time.

Once the storyboard is finished, it's time to start animating. The storyboard will serve as a reference for the animator as they create the animation. It will help the animator stay on track and ensure that all the elements of the animation are in place.

Storyboarding is an important part of the 3D animation process, and it's a skill that all animators should master. With the right software and a bit of practice, you can create professional-looking storyboards that will help to ensure the success of your animation.

CHAPTER FIVE

Modeling

Modeling is the process of creating three-dimensional representations of objects or environments. A 3D model is a digital representation of any object or environment that can be manipulated and animated in a virtual world. Modeling is an essential part of the 3D animation process and is the basis for creating believable and lifelike animations.

The modeling process begins with a concept, which is then translated into a 3D representation. This is usually done using specialized 3D modeling software. Models can be created from scratch or by using existing models and modifying them. The modeler will decide on the size, shape, texture, and other aspects of the model in order to create the desired results.

There are many different types of modeling techniques that can be used to create a 3D model. Polygonal modeling is the most common technique used in 3D animation. This technique uses polygons to create the shape of the model. Other techniques such as spline modeling, NURBS modeling, and sub-division modeling are also used.

Once the model has been created, it is then textured. Texturing is the process of applying colors and textures to the model to give it a realistic look. This is usually done using specialized 3D texturing software.

Once the model is complete, it can then be animated. This is done using keyframing or motion capture. In keyframing, the model is moved frame by frame to create a realistic animation. Motion capture is the process of capturing the motion of a real object and then applying it to the 3D model.

Modeling is an important part of the 3D animation process and requires a great deal of skill. Modelers must have an eye for detail and be able to understand the principles of 3D animation. With the help of 3D modeling software, modelers can create realistic and lifelike models that can be used in 3D animation.

CHAPTER SIX

Texturing and Lighting

Texturing and lighting are two of the most important aspects of 3D animation. Without good texturing and lighting, your 3D animation won't look as realistic and will lack the visual impact it needs to stand out.

Texturing can be used in a variety of ways, from adding realistic textures to a 3D model to adding a unique stylistic look to an animation. Texturing is an art form in itself and there are a variety of techniques that can be used to create different looks. Some of the most popular techniques include bump mapping, displacement mapping, normal mapping, and environment mapping.

Lighting is also essential for a realistic 3D animation. Without good lighting, your 3D models will look flat and uninteresting. You can use various lighting techniques to create different looks, such as ambient lighting, directional lighting, point lighting, and area lighting. Different light colors and intensities can also be used to create different moods and feelings.

Finally, compositing is the process of combining multiple elements of an animation into a single image. This can include adding visual effects, such as fog, smoke, or explosions, as well as combining multiple rendered frames into a single image. Compositing is a great way to add more realism and visual interest to your 3D animation.

Texturing and lighting play a major role in creating a realistic and visually appealing 3D animation. With the right techniques, you can create a unique and stunning animation that will be sure to impress your viewers.

CHAPTER SEVEN

Animation

Animation has come a long way since the days of traditional 2D animation. With the advent of 3D animation, artists and animators can bring their creations to life with a level of realism and detail that was previously impossible. In this chapter, we'll discuss the basics of 3D animation and how it is used in the modern world.

3D animation involves the use of computer-generated objects, known as 3D models, to create a simulated environment. It has become increasingly popular in the entertainment industry, with films and video games making extensive use of it. To create a 3D animation, an animator must first build the 3D model. This is done using specialized software such as Autodesk Maya, 3DS Max, and Blender. The model is then manipulated with animation software such as Adobe After Effects or Adobe Animate.

Once the model is complete, the animator can add movement to it. This is typically done by setting key frames and then manipulating the model between the frames. This process is known as "keyframing." Animators can also use motion capture technology to record the movement of real-life objects and apply it to their 3D models.

Finally, the animator can add various effects to the animation to make it look more realistic. These effects include shadows, lighting, textures, and motion blur. Once the animation is complete, it can be rendered and exported to various formats, such as MP4 and AVI.

3D animation has become a critical part of the entertainment industry. It has been used to create groundbreaking films such as Avatar and The Lord of the Rings trilogy, and video games such as Grand Theft Auto V and Fallout 4. With the increasing sophistication of 3D animation software, the possibilities are virtually limitless.

CHAPTER EIGHT

Rendering and Compositing

Rendering and compositing are two of the most important aspects of 3D animation. Rendering is producing a finished, photo-realistic image or animation from a 3D scene. Compositing is the process of combining two or more images into a single image or animation.

Rendering is taking a 3D scene and creating a final image or animation from it. This is done by rendering each frame of the animation individually, which can take anywhere from a few minutes to several hours, depending on the complexity and quality of the scene.

The rendering process involves translating the 3D scene into a 2D image, using various techniques such as ray tracing, global illumination, and ambient occlusion. Once a frame of the animation is rendered, it is combined with the other animation frames to create the final image or animation.

Compositing is the process of combining two or more images into a single image or animation. This is often done to add effects or to combine characters or elements from different scenes into a single scene.

Various techniques are used in compositing, such as rotoscoping, masking, and color grading. Rendering and compositing are important skills to master when creating 3D animations.

By understanding the principles and techniques of these two processes, animators are able to create more realistic and visually appealing animations.

CHAPTER NINE

Sound Design

Sound design is an integral part of 3D animation. It's the process of creating and manipulating sound to enhance the visual experience of an animation. The combination of sound and visuals can create an immersive experience for viewers and can be used to add atmosphere and emotion to a scene.

Sound design can be divided into two categories: Foley and sound effects. Foley is the art of creating realistic sound effects for an animation. This includes creating the sound of footsteps, doors opening, and other every day noises. Sound effects, on the other hand, are pre-recorded or synthesized effects that are used to create a more dynamic soundscape. These can include explosions, laser blasts, and other unnatural effects.

When creating sound design for an animation, it's important to consider how the sound will interact with the visuals. The sound should fit the atmosphere of the scene and should be used to draw the viewer in. It's also important to keep the sound design balanced and not overwhelming.

The best way to approach sound design is to start with a plan. Determine what types of sounds will be used in the animation and how they will be used to enhance the visuals. Once the plan is in place, the sound designer can start creating sound effects and adding them to the animation.

When working with sound, it's important to understand the basics of sound editing and mixing. Understanding the basics of sound will help the sound designer create a cohesive soundscape and make sure all the elements of the sound design are balanced. Sound design is an important part of 3D animation and can help to create an immersive experience for viewers.

By understanding the basics of sound design and planning ahead, sound designers can create a soundscape that will bring the animation to life.

Conclusion

We hope that this book has provided you with a strong understanding of the techniques and tools used in 3D animation. By understanding the fundamentals of 3D animation, you can now begin to create your own stunning digital images and animations. Good luck, and have fun!

9 798889 093688

Printed by Libri Plureos GmbH in Hamburg,
Germany